ON THE EUCHARIST AND THE LITURGY

THE EARLY CHURCH TODAY SERIES

Volume 3

The early leaders of the Church, tasked with shepherding Christ's flock, left us spiritual wealth that is too often neglected in modern times. The Early Church Today Series, published by the St. Mary & St. Moses Abbey Press, aims to help make that richness more accessible to readers, inviting them to see the applicability of the early Church to our walk with God today. By sharing practical selections from the writings of the early Church, aided by meaningful editorial supplements and revisions, each book will attempt to diminish impediments and bring to light what the Church has to offer.

The Early Church Today Series

ST. CYRIL OF JERUSALEM

ON THE EUCHARIST AND THE LITURGY

Edited & with an Introduction by

John Habib

On the Eucharist and the Liturgy
By St. Cyril of Jerusalem

Designed & Published by:
St. Mary & St. Moses Abbey Press
101 S Vista Dr, Sandia, TX 78383
stmabbeypress.com

Source of St. Cyril's lectures, unless otherwise noted, derived from the translation overseen by Philip Schaff in the Nicene and Post-Nicene Fathers (*Nicene and Post-Nicene Fathers: Second Series* 9, Philip Schaff, ed. (1886–1889; repr. New York, NY: Cosimo, Inc., 2007), and was further revised as minimally as possible to replace archaic words with modern equivalents, and to implement syntactic improvements.

Library of Congress Control Number: 2024938063

Cover art and illustrations derived from images by Tasony Sawsan.

CONTENTS

Introduction

LIFE OF ST. CYRIL OF JERUSALEM

Born a few years before the infamous heresy of Arian, which led to the gathering of bishops at the ecumenical council of Nicaea in AD 325, he eventually took part in the next ecumenical council in Constantinople in AD 381. Little is known about his life. Various hagiographies, including the Coptic Synaxarion, make mention of his early years as having been raised with a Christian upbringing. His teachings about parents generally may have been inspired by his gratitude to his own: "The first virtue of godliness in Christians is to honor their parents, to repay them for their trouble, and with all their power to confer on them what will lead to their comfort, for however much we should repay them, yet we will never be able to return to them what they as parents have been to us."[1]

St. Cyril's early years were lived during the reign of Emperor Constantine, after the emperor's conversion to Christianity (who is even said to have gifted St. Cyril a valuable robe fashioned with gold thread, for him to wear when he performed the rite of baptism),[2] and as such he

1 Cyril of Jerusalem, Catechetical Lecture 7, Part 16. In *Nicene and Post-Nicene Fathers: Second Series* 7, Philip Schaff, ed. (1886–1889; repr. New York, NY: Cosimo, Inc., 2007) (henceforth, when cited, will be referred to as NPNF²).

2 Drijvers, Jan Willem, *Cyril of Jerusalem: Bishop and City.* Supplements to Vigiliae Christianae, Volume 72 (Leiden, NL: Brill, 2004), 65.

had an opportunity to live at a time of relative peace during the first part of his life, until he found himself the target of persecution from those who were still fond of Arianism, leading to his exile three times from his See in Jerusalem. It was not until the death of the Arian emperor Valens (c. AD 378) that St. Cyril was able to return to his See until his departure in AD 386.[1]

St. Cyril was ordained a deacon by the bishop of Jerusalem,[2] and then later ordained a priest at some time in the early 340s. A few years later, estimated to be around the year 348, he was entrusted with the responsibility to teach catechumens (Christian converts being given oral instruction [catechesis][3] in the faith, before baptism). Having been assigned to this important role, we see how well regarded he was among his peers, which was later affirmed when he was chosen to succeed Bishop Maximus in the See of Jerusalem around AD 350.[4]

In the first year of St. Cyril's episcopate, during the reign of Emperor Constantius (the son of Emperor Constantine the Great), St. Cyril describes (in a letter to Constantius) a

1 Introduction to the Life of St. Cyril, Chapter 1 (NPNF[2] page xi)

2 Based on a remark by St. Jerome (c. AD 347–420) in his *Chronicles*, it is inferred that the bishop who ordained St. Cyril a deacon was Macarius, Bishop of Jerusalem, and then his successor, Bishop Maximus, ordained St. Cyril as a priest.

3 This is derived from a Greek word, meaning "oral instruction."

4 This is approximately determined by St. Cyril's letter to Constantius, written in AD 351, in which he referred to his the miracle of the appearance of a luminous cross in the sky at Jerusalem as the first-fruit of his episcopate. Thus, he must have been ordained as a bishop in 350 or early 351.

miracle seen by innumerable witnesses in the city of Jerusalem, of a cross of light in heaven for an extended length of time. It is worthwhile to share portions of St. Cyril's own account of this miracle of "the sign which appeared in the sky":

> ... In the time of your blessed father Constantine ... the saving wood of the Cross was found in Jerusalem when God's grace rewarded the piety of his noble search with the discovery of the hidden holy places.... But you, ... in your time miracles have now appeared ... in the heavens: the trophy of the victory which our Lord and Savior Jesus Christ, the Only-begotten Son of God, won over death—I refer to the blessed cross—has been seen flashing like lightning over Jerusalem.
>
> In these holy days of the Easter season,[1] on May 7, at about the third hour, a huge cross made of light appeared in the sky above holy Golgotha extending as far as the holy Mount of Olives. It was not revealed to one or two people alone, but it appeared unmistakably to everyone in the city. It was not as if one might conclude that one had suffered a momentary optical illusion; it was visible to the human eye above the earth for several hours. The flashes it emitted outshone the rays of the sun, which would have outshone and obscured it themselves if it had not presented the watchers with a more powerful illumination than the

1 The fifty holy days following the feast of the Resurrection until the day of Pentecost (the day on which the Church celebrates the descent of the of the Holy Spirit upon the disciples and many other followers who were gathered to pray).

> sun. It prompted the whole populate at once to run together into the holy church, overcome both with fear and joy at the divine vision. Young and old, men and women of every age, even young girls confined to their rooms at home, natives and foreigners, Christians and pagans visiting from abroad, all together as if with a single voice raised a hymn of praise to God's Only-begotten Son the wonder-worker. They had the evidence of their own senses that the holy faith of Christians is not based on the persuasive arguments of philosophy but on the revelation of the Spirit and power; it is not proclaimed by mere human beings but testified from heaven by God himself. Accordingly, we citizens of Jerusalem who saw this extraordinary wonder with our own eyes, have paid due worship and thanksgiving to God...[1]

The miracle of the appearance of the cross of light above Golgotha is commemorated by the Coptic Church on the 12th of the Coptic month of Pashons (corresponding to May 20; this miracle is commemorated in the Byzantine rite on May 7).[2]

The Coptic Church commemorates the departure of St. Cyril on the 22nd of the Coptic month of Paremhotep (which corresponds to March 31; in the Roman and Byzantine rites, he is commemorated on March 18).

---

1 Edward Yarnold, *Cyril of Jerusalem* (New York, NY: Routledge, 2000), 68–70.

2 The letter by St. Cyril is dated May 7, 351.

CATECHETICAL LECTURES OF ST. CYRIL

St. Cyril's catechetical lectures were given (as noted above) while St. Cyril was serving as a priest, just a few years before he was chosen as the bishop of Jerusalem. Candidates for baptism in the early Church commonly would undergo a probationary period, being instructed in the Christian faith; this follows the prescribed caution to ensure genuine allegiance to God, as the Christian convert and prolific Latin Christian writer Tertullian (c. AD 160-230) states: "They whose office it is [to administer baptism], know that baptism is not rashly to be administered."[1] During this period of instruction (which commonly occurred during the forty days of fasting before the Feast of the Resurrection), catechumens would usually also practice ascetical discipline, whereby "those who are coming to baptism," Tertullian tells us, "must be constantly engaged in prayers, fasting, kneeling, and watching, together with confession of all past faults."[2] As such, we find that St. Cyril states in his initial opening lecture (the protocatechesis, or prologue to the catechetical lectures): "A long notice is allowed for you—you have forty days for repentance; you have full opportunity both to put off [the old garment], and wash, and to put on [a new garment—'the brightest robe of chastity'] and enter [the wedding feast with Christ the Bridegroom])"; following his introductory lectures, he ventures in more detailed teaching regarding

1 Tertullian, *On Baptism*, 18. In *The Ante-Nicene Fathers* 3, Alexander Roberts and James Donaldson, eds. (Buffalo, NY: The Christian Literature Company, 1885) (hereinafter referred to as ANF).

2 Tertullian, *On Baptism*, 20. ANF 3.

repentance and remissions of sins, and about our adversary (Satan), before embarking on the substantive topics for the remainder of his lectures. His lectures are divided in two main segments:

- The first consists of 18 lectures on what one needs to know in order to be baptized (regarding repentance, baptism, faith, and a detailed walkthrough of the Creed [lectures 7–18]), after which those who were admitted to be baptized would follow the ancient and well-attested early Church rite of the baptism ceremony, facing the west and renouncing Satan and all his works, followed by turning towards the east and professing their faith (reciting the Creed).[1]
- The second segment consists of five lectures for those who have just been newly baptized, teaching about the mysteries of baptism, chrismation, the Eucharist (the partaking of the body and blood of Christ), and the Divine Liturgy.

It is the last two of St. Cyril's lectures that make up the majority of this book. As the early Church consistently taught

1 In the *Apostolic Constitutions,* the candidate is required to recite the whole Creed immediately after the renunciation after Satan: "And after his renunciation let him...say: 'And I associate myself to Christ, and believe and am baptized into One Unbegotten Being, the Only True God Almighty, the Father of Christ, ... and into the Lord Jesus Christ ... and I am baptized into the Holy Spirit, ... into the resurrection of the flesh, and into the remission of sins, and into the Kingdom of heaven, and into the life of the world to come.' And after this vow, he comes in order to the anointing with oil [i.e., chrismation]." (7.41 ANF 7:476)

clearly: baptism and chrismation, administered by those who have been granted the authority to do so,[1] allows one to then partake of the Eucharist, which is offered during the Divine Liturgy, which is the path for eternal life and salvation which is ultimately St. Cyril's aim and purpose:

> When therefore you renounce Satan, utterly breaking … your covenant with him, that ancient league with hell, there is opened to you the Paradise of God, which He planted towards the east, when for his transgression our first father was banished.[2]
>
> Then may the gate of Paradise be opened to every man and every woman among you. Then may you enjoy the Christ-bearing waters in their fragrance. Then may you receive the name of Christ, and the power of things divine…. Great is the baptism that

---

1 This is within the "bishop's authority" (Tertullian, *On Baptism,* 17. ANF 3) who have in turn derived their ordination by successive ordination traced back to the time of the apostles (as evinced in Scripture, and the early Church [e.g., Irenaeus, Tertullian, Cyprian of Carthage]): "He cannot be reckoned as a bishop who succeeds no one. For he has despised the evangelical and apostolic tradition, springing from himself. For he who has not been ordained in the Church can neither have nor hold to the Church in any way…. How can he be esteemed a pastor who succeeds no one, but begins from himself? For the true shepherd remains and presides over the church of God by successive ordination. Therefore, the other one becomes a stranger and a profane person, an enemy of the Lord's peace." (Cyprian of Carthage, Epistle 75, Part 3. In ANF 5). See also the Epistle of Ignatius to the Smyrnaeans, where in Part 8 he describes how the Eucharist must be administered by the bishop, or one to whom the bishop has entrusted it (e.g., priests).

2 Cyril of Jerusalem, Catechetical Lecture 19.9. In Gerard Luttikhuizen, *Paradise Interpreted: Representations of Biblical Paradise in Judaism and Christianity* (Leiden, NL: Brill, 1999), 155.

lies before you: a ransom to captives; a remission of offenses; a death of sin; a new-birth of the soul; a garment of light; a holy indissoluble seal; a chariot to heaven; the delight of Paradise; a welcome into the kingdom; the gift of adoption!

I have long been wishing, O true-born and dearly beloved children of the Church … [that] I might lead you by the hand into the brighter and more fragrant meadow of the Paradise before us; especially as you have been made fit to receive the more sacred mysteries [the body and blood of Christ] after having been found worthy of divine and life-giving baptism.[1]

NOTES REGARDING CHAPTER 1
(Ready Yourself for Partaking of the Eucharist)

St. Cyril's lectures from which most of this chapter was derived are taken from his prologue to his catechetical lectures (protocatechesis). As such, although the focus was as an introduction to the lectures the catechumens were about to hear, much of what he said is insightful as an instruction that can be applied to those who are gathering in church for solemn purposes, including the Divine Liturgy.

1 Cyril of Jerusalem, Catechetical Lecture *Procatechesis* 15–16. Ibid., 154.

NOTES REGARDING CHAPTER 2
(On the Mystery of the Body and the Blood of Christ)

St. Cyril consistently teaches that the mysteries require the invocation of the Holy Spirit, after which the water of baptism is no longer simply water,[1] the oil (of chrismation) no longer plain oil, and the bread and the wine are no longer plain bread and wine, but the body and blood of Christ.[2] The "unfaltering faith" in the mystery of the Eucharist is required: "Do not trust your bodily palate's judgment; no, rather your unfaltering faith, for they who taste are asked to taste, not bread and wine, but the … body and blood of Christ."[3] This is not novel theology or doctrine, but rather consistently taught, beginning with Scripture (read Christ's teachings in the Gospel of John [Chapter 6] and St. Paul's mention of the gravity of the mystery in his first epistle to the Corinthians [Chapter 10 and 11]), and in the writings of the early Church (for example, Ignatius of Antioch around [c. AD 105],[4] Irenaeus [c. AD 180],[5] Clement of Alexandria

1 Cyril of Jerusalem, Catechetical Lecture 3, Part 3.

2 Ibid., Lecture 21, Part 3 and Part 7.

3 Ibid., Lecture 23, Part 20.

4 "[Some] abstain from the Eucharist and from prayer, because they do not believe the Eucharist to be the flesh of our Savior Jesus Christ.… Those, therefore, who speak against this gift of God, incur death." *Epistle to the Symrnaeans* 7, ANF 1.

5 "[The wine and bread] having received the Word of God, become the Eucharist, which is the body and blood of Christ." *Against Heresies* 5.2.2.

[c. AD 195],[1] and Origen [c. AD 248]).[2]

NOTES REGARDING CHAPTER 3
(On the Holy Liturgy)

In the last chapter of this book, additional content is provided as a reference and editorial supplement to St. Cyril's lecture. As he walks us through the liturgical rites and prayers at his time, the modern day correlated liturgical text is presented, with accompanying commentary to draw out the parallels between the two, and provide further clarity and context.

1 "To drink the blood of Jesus is to become a partaker of the Lord's immortality.... As wine is blended with water, so is the Spirit with man ... And the mixture of both—of the water and of the Word—is called the Eucharist, renowned and glorious grace. Those who by faith partake of it are sanctified both in body and soul." *The Instructor (Paedagogus)* 2, ANF 2.

2 "We also eat the bread presented to us. And this bread becomes by prayer a sacred body, which sanctifies those who sincerely partake of it." *Against Celsus (Contra Celsum)* 33, ANF 4.

We adopted the partitioning of the source text (see copyright page for reference).

5 Then the Priest says, "Let us give thanks to the Lord." For verily we are bound to give thanks, that He called us, unworthy as we were, to so great grace; that He reconciled us when we were His foes; that He granted to us the Spirit of adoption. Then you say, "It is meet and right," for in giving thanks we do a meet thing and a right thing. But He did not just do right, but more than right, in doing us good and counting us for such great benefits.

THE ANAPHORA

Turning to the west, the priest signs the people once with the sign of the cross, saying:

Priest:
The Lord be with you all.

Congregation:
And with your spirit.

The priest turns to the East and signs the deacons on his right once with the sign of the cross, saying:

Priest:
Lift up your hearts.

Congregation:
We have them with the Lord.

The priest signs himself once with the sign of the cross, saying:

Priest:
Let us give thanks to the Lord.

Congregation:
It is meet and right.

Editor's Commentary

In the Liturgy, the Church still retains this very ancient segment of the service, referred to as the "Anaphora," which is a Greek word (ἀναφορά) meaning "Lifting up," corresponding to the first declaration of the Priest to all present: "Lift up your hearts."

All the components of the Anaphora, and the responses back and forth, are present still in the Liturgy used in the church today, just as St. Cyril described it during his time.

Commentary by the editor is provided, to draw out the parallels between St. Cyril's lectures and the modern liturgical rite in the Coptic Orthodox Church, and to provide further clarity and context.

The most commonly used liturgical text in the Coptic Orthodox Church, known as the Liturgy of St. Basil the Great, is provided, in correlation to St. Cyril's mention of the liturgical rites and prayers during his time. The remarkable similarity between the two is evident throughout.

Note: see the next page for more detail on particular terminology used in the "Editor's Commentary."

Note: prayers in italics indicate an "inaudible" prayer.

In the "Editor's Commentary" there are certain terms used, with specific meanings intended for the purposes of this book:

- **Liturgy.** When capitalized, this refers to the most commonly used liturgical text in the Coptic Orthodox Church, known as the Liturgy of St. Basil the Great.[1]

- **Priest.** This term is used to refer to the priest or the bishop—the clergyman—who officiates the service during the Liturgy.

- **Deacon.** This term will be applied here to refer generally to any rank of the diaconate (chanter, reader, subdeacon, deacon or archdeacon); in the Coptic Church, it is commonplace to use the term "deacon" in such a way. Despite this, it is worthwhile to note that the true title of "deacon" is actually reserved for a very select few who can be regarded as similar to the rank given to the very first deacons in the book of Acts. More formally then, the Church rank of "deacon," ranking below a priest, has been around since the time of the apostles, being instituted by them (see Acts 6) and attested to elsewhere in the Bible (1 Tim 3:8–13; Phil 1:1). They differ from priests and bishops in that they are not able to invoke the

1 The text is derived from the following liturgical book source: *The Divine Liturgies of Saints Basil, Gregory, and Cyril* (Tallahassee, FL: St. Mary & St. George Coptic Orthodox Church, Coptic Orthodox Diocese of the Southern United States, 2001).

Holy Spirit to effectuate any of the Church mysteries. The blessed Ignatius (who was a personal disciple of one or more of the apostles) distinguishes between the three principal ranks (referred to by some as "Major Orders") of the Church—bishop, priest, and deacon—and states (c. AD 105), "apart from these there is no Church."[1] Chanters, readers, and subdeacons are hierarchically below the rank of deacon.

- **Church.** As applied in this chapter, references to the "Church" (capitalized) will mean the Coptic Orthodox Church. If any other meaning is intended, it will be written in a manner that should be understood by its context and phrasing (for example, the use of the term "early Church.")

Finally, as St. Cyril stated at the opening of his teaching on the liturgy, we conclude: "And now it is necessary to pass on to what is next in order, meaning today, to set the crown on the spiritual building of your edification."[2]

---

1 David Bercot, *Dictionary of Early Christian Beliefs* (Peabody, MA: Hendrickson Publishers, Inc., 2010), 158 (quoting Ignatius Epistle to the Trallians 3 [ANF 1:67]).

2 Cyril of Jerusalem, Catechetical Lecture 23, Part 1.

CHAPTER ONE

Ready Yourself for Partaking of the Eucharist

PROCATECHESIS

1 The honesty of purpose makes you called, for if your body is here but not your mind, it profits you nothing...."

***

3 A certain man in the Gospels once was curious about the marriage feast[1] and took an unbecoming garment, and came in, sat down, and ate, because the bridegroom permitted it. But when he saw them all dressed in white, he ought to have put on a garment of the same kind himself. Considering that he partook of the same food, but was unlike them in clothing style and in purpose. The bridegroom, however, although

1 Matthew 22

benevolent, was not undiscerning. And in going around to each of the guests and observing them (because his care was not about their eating, but about their appropriate behavior), he saw a stranger "who did not have on a wedding garment"[1] and said to him: "Friend, how did you come in here?"[2] In what an [unbecoming] color, with what a conscience! Even though the doorkeeper did not forbid you, yet because of the benevolence of the host? Even though you were ignorant about what clothing style you should come in to the banquet, you did come in and did see the glitter fashions of the guests, yet should you not have been taught even by what was before your eyes? Should you not have withdrawn in an opportune time, so you can enter again when suitable? But now you have come in unsuitably, to be inopportunely cast out. So he commands the servants, "Bind his feet" which daringly intruded, "Bind his hands" which did not know how to put a bright garment around himself, and "cast him into outer darkness," for he is unworthy of the wedding torches.[3] You see what happened to that man? Make your own condition safe."

4 For we, the ministers of Christ, have admitted everyone, and occupying, as it were, the place of doorkeepers, we left the door open; and possibly you entered with your soul bemired with sins, and with a defiled will. Yet you did enter, and

1 Matthew 22:12

2 Ibid.

3 This may refer to the supposed torches or lighted tapers that candidates for baptism would hold during a procession as they are admitted as catechumens [as noted in Procatechesis 1: "Thus far there has been an inscription of your names, and a call to service, and torches of the bridal train, and a longing for heavenly citizenship, and a good purpose, and hope afterward."

were allowed; your name was inscribed. Tell me, did you behold this venerable constitution of the Church? Did you view her order and discipline,[1] the reading of Scriptures, the presence of the ordained,[2] the course of instructions? Be humbled by the place, and be taught by what you see. Go out at an opportune time now, and enter at an opportune time tomorrow.

If the garment of your soul is greed, put on another garment and come in. Put off your former garment, do not cover it up. Put off, I implore you, fornication and uncleanness, and put on the brightest robe of chastity. This charge I give you, before Jesus the Bridegroom of souls comes in and sees their attire. A long notice [period] is allowed to you; you have forty days for repentance,[3] you have full opportunity both to put off [your garment], and wash, and to put on [another garment] and enter. But if you persist in an evil purpose, the speaker is blameless... If anyone is conscious of his wound, let him take the ointment; if any have fallen, let him arise. Let there be ... no hypocrisy, no idle curiosity about the matter.

5 Possibly too you have come on another pretext. It is possible

1 The word here (in Greek, ἐπιστήμη [epistēmē], which commonly means "knowledge" or "understanding") may be regarded to have a similar meaning to the word "rite," applied here to describe the intelligence and skill displayed in the arrangement of the public services of the Church. Consider for comparison the Apostolic Constitutions (2.57), where the bishop is told to have the assemblies arranged with all knowledge (μετὰ πάσης ἐπιστήμη [meta pasēs epistēmē]), which may be understood to say, "arranged in accordance with the rites / traditions passed down to us."

2 What is meant here includes the clergy, diaconate, monks, etc.

3 This was referencing the 40 days of the fast prior to the Feast of the Resurrection.

that a man is wishing to pursue a woman, and come here on that account. The remark applies in like manner to women also in their turn.... I accept this bait for the hook, and welcome you, though you came with an evil purpose, yet as one to be saved by a good hope. Perhaps you do not know why you were coming, nor in what kind of net you are being taken up. You came in with the Church's nets; be taken alive, do not flee, for Jesus is fishing for you, not in order to kill, but by killing to make alive, for you must die and rise again. For you have heard the Apostle say, "dead indeed to sin, but living unto righteousness."[1] Die to your sins, and live to righteousness; live from this very day.

LECTURE 4

29 But let your apparel be plain, not for adornment, but for necessary covering; not to minister to your vanity, but to keep you warm in winter, and to hide the unseemliness of the body, in case under the pretense of hiding your unseemliness, you fall into another kind of unseemliness by your extravagant clothing.

1 Cf. Romans 6:11, 14

CHAPTER TWO

On the Mystery of the Body and the Blood of Christ

LECTURE 21

3 "... the bread of the Eucharist, after the invocation of the Holy Spirit, is mere bread no longer, but the body of Christ."

LECTURE 22

1 Even of itself the teaching of the blessed Paul is sufficient to give you a full assurance concerning those Divine Mysteries, of which, having been deemed worthy, you have become of the same body and blood with Christ. For you have just heard him say distinctly, "That our Lord Jesus Christ in the night in which He was betrayed, took bread, and when He had given thanks He broke it, and gave to His disciples, saying, 'Take, eat, this is My body,' and having taken the cup and

given thanks, He said, 'Take, drink, this is My blood.'"[1] Since then He Himself declared and said of the bread, "This is My body," who shall dare to doubt any longer? And since He has Himself affirmed and said, "This is My blood," who shall ever hesitate, saying, that it is not His blood?

2 He once in Cana of Galilee turned the water into wine, akin to blood, and is it incredible that He should have turned wine into blood? When called to a bodily marriage, He miraculously wrought that wonderful work; and "on the children of the bridechamber,"[2] shall He not much rather be acknowledged to have bestowed the fruition of His Body and Blood?

3 Therefore with full assurance let us partake of the body and blood of Christ, for in the figure[3] of bread is given to you His body, and in the figure of wine His blood, so that you, by partaking of the body and blood of Christ, may be made of the same body and the same blood with Him. For thus we come to bear Christ in us, because His body and blood are distributed through our members; thus it is that, according to the blessed Peter, we become partakers of the divine nature.[4]

4 Christ on a certain occasion discoursing with the Jews said, "Unless you eat My flesh and drink My blood, you have no life in you."[5] They not having heard His saying in a spiritual sense were offended, and went back, supposing that He was

---

1 1 Corinthians 11:23. Some variation to this passage may be attributed to inclusions from the account in Matthew 26:26.

2 Matthew 9:15

3 τύπος (*typos*)—"type"

4 2 Peter 1:4

5 John 6:53

inviting them to eat flesh.

5 In the Old Testament also there was showbread, but that,[1] as it belonged to the Old Testament, has come to an end. But in the New Testament there is the bread of heaven, and a cup of salvation, sanctifying soul and body, for as the bread corresponds to our body, so is the Word[2] appropriate to our soul.

6 Consider therefore the bread and the wine not as bare elements, for they are, according to the Lord's declaration, the body and blood of Christ; for even though sense suggests this to you, yet let faith establish you. Judge not the matter from the taste, but from faith be fully assured without misgiving, that the body and blood of Christ have been granted to you.

7 Also the blessed David shall advise you the meaning of this, saying, "You have prepared a table before me in the presence of those that afflict me."[3] What he says is to this effect: "Before Your coming, the evil spirits prepared a table for men, polluted and defiled and full of devilish influence;[4] but since Your Coming O Lord, 'You have prepared a table

---

1 Exodus 25:23–30; Leviticus 24:5–9

2 *Logos* (λόγος), referring to Christ (see also the Gospel of John, Chapter 1)

3 Psalm 23:5

4 St. Cyril refers to idolatrous feasts which St. Paul discusses in 1 Corinthians 10:14, 18–22 (considering the sacrifices offered to idols as a "table of demons"; St. Paul also indicates that even if someone is invited to a guest's house and is offered food that was previously offered to idols, to not eat of it [1 Corinthians 10:28]). This was of such concern that it was one of the main decrees from the council at Jerusalem, where the apostles gathered to discuss pressing issues they were facing, declaring by a letter: "For it seemed good to the Holy Spirit, and to us, to lay upon you no greater burden than these necessary things" among which they listed "that you abstain from things offered to idols" (Acts 15:28–29).

before me.'" When the man says to God, "You have prepared a table before me," what else does he indicate other than that mystical and spiritual table, which God has prepared for us in contrast, that is, contrary and in opposition to the evil spirits? And very truly, for that [former table] had communion with devils, but this [spiritual table], with God. "You anointed my head with oil"[1]—With oil He anointed your head, upon your forehead, for the seal[2] which you have of God, that you may be made the engraving of the signet, "Holiness unto God."[3] "And your cup intoxicates me, as [a] very strong [drink]"[4]—You see that cup here spoken of, which Jesus took in His hands, and gave thanks, and said, "This is My blood, which

1 Psalm 23:5

2 This seal refers to the Mystery of Chrismation, by which the Holy Spirit is invoked to enter into a person at some point after baptism, making that person a new creation (2 Corinthians 5:17) and a child of God (Galatians 4), whereby they become a "temple of the Holy Spirit" (1 Corinthians 6:19). It is called chrismation, being derived from the Greek word *chrisma*, which means "anointing," because the newly baptized is anointed with holy oil—*myron* (a Greek word referring to fragrant oil)—to effectuate this mystery through the Holy Spirit. This was established in accompaniment or in lieu of the original manner by which the Holy Spirit used to be relayed to the newly baptized—the laying on of hands—at some point very early on in the history of Christianity.

3 In Exodus 28:36–38, we see that God directs Aaron the priest to wear on his head a headplate of pure gold, engraved with the words "Holy to the Lord." ("And you shall make a plate of pure gold, and engrave on it, like the engraving of a signet, 'Holy to the Lord.' And you shall fasten it on the turban by a lace of blue; it shall be on the front of the turban. It shall be upon Aaron's forehead ..." [RSV]). St. Cyril transfers this symbolism to the Christian who has been sealed by the Myron and has become a holy temple of God.

4 This translation of Psalm 23:5 is derived from the Septuagint, the Old Testament as written in Greek and available to the early fathers such as St. Cyril.

is shed for many for the remission of sins."[1]

8 Therefore Solomon also, hinting at this grace, says in Ecclesiastes: "Come here, eat your bread with joy" (that is, the spiritual bread; "come here"—he calls with the call to salvation and blessing), "and drink your wine with a merry heart" (that is, the spiritual wine). "And let oil be poured out upon your head" (you see he alludes even to the mystical Chrism), "and let your garments be always white, for the Lord is well pleased with your works,"[2] for before you come to Baptism, your works were "vanity of vanities."[3] But now, having put off your old garments, and put on those which are spiritually white, you must be continually robed in white; of course we mean not this, that you are always to wear white raiment. But you must be clad in the garments that are truly white and shining and spiritual, that you may say with the blessed Isaiah, "My soul shall be joyful in my God, for He has clothed me with a garment of salvation, and put a robe of gladness around me."[4]

9 Having learned these things, and been fully assured that the seeming bread is not bread, though sensible to taste, but the body of Christ; and that the seeming wine is not wine, though the taste will have it so, but the blood of Christ; and that of this David sung of old, saying, "and bread strengthens man's heart, to make his face to shine with oil"[5] ("strengthen your heart," by partaking thereof as spiritual, and "make the

1 Matthew 26:28

2 Ecclesiastes 9:7–8

3 Ecclesiastes 1:2

4 Isaiah 61:10

5 Psalm 104:15

face of your soul shine." And so having it unveiled with a pure conscience, may you "reflect as a mirror the glory of the Lord,"[1] and proceed from "glory to glory,"[2] in Christ Jesus our Lord, to whom be honor, and might, and glory, forever and ever.

1 2 Corinthians 3:18

2 Ibid.

CHAPTER THREE

On the Holy Liturgy

LECTURE 23

1 By the loving-kindness of God you have heard sufficiently at our former meetings concerning Baptism, and Chrismation,[1] and partaking of the body and blood of Christ,[2] and now it is necessary to pass on to what is next in order, meaning today, to set the crown on the spiritual building of your edification.

2 You have seen then the deacon who gives to the priest water to wash, and to the presbyters who stand around God's altar. He gave it not at all because of bodily defilement; it is not that, for we did not enter the Church at first with defiled bodies. But the washing of hands is a symbol that you ought to be

1 St. Cyril gave these lectures in former meetings with catechumens being instructed in the faith, on Baptism (Lecture 20) and Chrismation (Lecture 21), and these were not included in this book, which focuses on the Eucharist and the Liturgy.

2 See Chapter 2

pure from all sinful and unlawful deeds, for since the hands are a symbol of action, by washing them, it is evident, we represent the purity and blamelessness of our conduct. Did you not hear the blessed David opening this very mystery and saying, "I will wash my hands in innocence, and so will I go about Your Altar, O Lord." The washing therefore of hands is a symbol of freedom from sin.

THE ORTHODOX CREED

Congregation:

We believe in one God, God the Father, the Pantocrator ...

The people chant the last sentence in a loud voice:

We look for the resurrection of the dead, and the life of the age to come. Amen.

During the above chant, the priest washes his hands three times at the north side of the altar, saying the first time:

Priest:

You shall sprinkle me with hyssop, and I shall be purified; You shall wash me, and I shall be made whiter than snow. [Ps. 50:7]

The second time, he says:

You shall make me to hear joyfulness and gladness; the humbled bones shall rejoice. [Ps. 50:8]

The third time, he says:

I will wash my hands in innocence, and go round about Your altar, O Lord, that I may hear the voice of Your praise. Alleluia. [Ps. 25:6,7].

Now the priest looks towards the west, shakes the water off his hands before all the people, then dries his hands with a clean towel:

Editor's Commentary

In the early church writing known as the Apostolic Constitutions (8.11), this duty is assigned to a subdeacon, but is nonetheless something ancient: "Let one of the subdeacons bring water to wash the hands of the priests, which is a symbol of the purity of those souls that are devoted to God."

Today in the Coptic Church rite, after the "Liturgy of the Word" (during which we read readings from the letters of St. Paul [the "Pauline epistle"], a "universal" letter by another New Testament author [also called the "Catholic"—meaning "universal"—epistle], the Book of Acts [also known by its Greek name "Praxis"), a reading from the Coptic Synaxarion (notable events and lives of saints in Church history), a Psalm and Gospel reading, and then often a sermon), we then begin the portion of the service known as the "Liturgy of the Faithful."

The Liturgy of the Faithful is called as such because in the early Church only the "faithful"—that is, Christians—would be in attendance. As such, the Christian faithful would

Priest:
Let us pray.

Deacon:
Stand up for prayer.

The priest bows to his brethren priests, and turns to the west and signs the people with the sign of the cross once, saying:

Priest:
Peace be with all.

Congregation:
And with your spirit.

begin this segment of the Liturgy by declaring their beliefs, reciting, out loud, the Orthodox Creed of Faith.

As the faithful chant the last sentence of the Creed ("We look for the resurrection of the dead, and the life of the age to come. Amen"), the priest washes his hands three times at the north side of the altar. Often, this will involve one of the members of the diaconate accompanying the priest to an area in the sanctuary which has a bowl or sink present, ready to catch water that a deacon pours from a vessel he is holding. During the first washing, the priest prays inaudibly: "You shall sprinkle me with hyssop, and I shall be purified; You shall wash me, and I shall be made whiter than snow" (Psalm 51:7). The second time he prays: "You shall make me to hear joyfulness and gladness; the humbled bones shall rejoice" (Psalm 51:8). The third time, he prays: "I will wash my hands in innocence, and go round about Your altar, O Lord, that I may hear the voice of Your praise. Alleluia" (Psalm 26:6,7] (Note that this is the *same* psalm that St. Cyril says the priests would pray during his time during the washing of hands; this rite is one the Coptic Church retains in its liturgical service).

Then the priest goes toward the front of the sanctuary, looks toward the west (in the direction of the congregation), shakes the water off his hands before all the people, and then dries his hands with a clean towel (held usually by a deacon, commonly the one who poured water on the priest's hands), ready to hand to the priest).

3 Then the deacon cries aloud, "Receive one another, and let us kiss one another." Think not that this kiss is of the same character with those given in public by common friends. It is not such; rather, this kiss blends souls one with another, and courts entire forgiveness for them. The kiss therefore is the sign that our souls are mingled together, and banish all remembrance of wrongs. For this reason Christ said, "If you

bring your gift at the altar, and there remember that your brother has something against you, leave your gift there upon the altar, and go your way. First be reconciled with your brother, and then come and offer your gift."[1] The kiss therefore is reconciliation, and for this reason holy, as the blessed Paul somewhere cried, saying, "Greet one another with a holy kiss,"[2] and Peter, with a "kiss of love."[3]

1 Matthew 5:23–24

2 1 Corinthians 16:20

3 1 Peter 5:14: "Greet one another with a kiss of love. Peace to you all who are in Christ Jesus. Amen."

THE PRAYER OF RECONCILIATION

Priest:
O God, the Great, the Eternal, who formed man in incorruption; and death, which entered into the world through the envy of the devil, You have destroyed by the life-giving manifestation of Your only-begotten Son, our Lord, God, and Savior Jesus Christ. You have filled the earth with the heavenly peace by which the host of angels glorify You, saying, "Glory to God in the highest, peace on earth, and good will towards men."

Deacon:
Pray for perfect peace, love, and the holy apostolic kisses.

Congregation:
Lord have mercy.

Priest:
According to Your good will, O God, fill our hearts with Your peace. Cleanse us from all blemish, all guile, all hypocrisy, all craftiness, and the remembrance of evil bearing death. And make us all worthy, O our Master, to greet one another with a

Editor's Commentary

After the Creed, and the washing of the priest's hands, the priest prays the "Reconciliation Prayer," recalling to people's memory the work of reconciliation between God and man, which God initiated by the life-giving manifestation of the Lord Jesus Christ. The priest concludes the reconciliation prayer by praying: "Make us all worthy, O our master, to greet one another with a holy kiss, that without casting us into condemnation, we partake of Your immortal and heavenly gift in Christ Jesus our Lord." This is then followed by the deacon directing the congregation to "Greet one another with a holy kiss."

The Church today retains all of the practices and spiritual meaning of those rites as St. Cyril describes. St. Cyril highlights "the kiss therefore is reconciliation," and also "for this reason [it is] holy." He reminds us that one must not partake of this holy kiss, that without casting us into condemnation we may partake of Your immortal and heavenly gift in Christ Jesus our Lord. *Through whom the glory, the honor, the dominion, and the worship are due unto You, with Him and the Holy Spirit, the Giver of Life, who is of one essence with You, now and at all times and unto the age of all ages. Amen.*

Then the deacon, holding the cross, says:

Deacon:
Greet one another with a holy kiss. Lord have mercy. Lord have mercy. Lord have mercy. Yea, Lord, who are Jesus Christ, the Son of God, hear us and have mercy upon us. Offer, [offer, offer] in order. Stand with trembling. Look towards the East. Let us attend.

"gift" unless they are at peace and have forgiven each other of "all remembrance of wrongs." This is what the priest today in the Church prays, seeking that we may greet one another "without condemnation" (that is, genuinely have forgiven all from everyone, and are not merely taking the action of greeting while one's heart is not clear from the remembrance of wrongs). The deacon in the Liturgy, during the reconciliation prayer, prays "for perfect peace, love, and the holy apostolic kisses," distinguishing between the genuine kisses of the apostles of Christ and the deceitful kiss of the former disciple Judas who betrayed his Master with a kiss that was not genuinely of peace and love. And thus, with a heart that loves and has forgiven everyone, one may "partake of [God's] ... heavenly gift," as the priest prays in the Liturgy.

4 After this the Priest cries aloud, "Lift up your hearts," for truly ought we in that most awful hour to have our heart on high with God, and not below, thinking of earth and earthly things. In effect therefore the Priest bids all in that hour to dismiss all cares of this life, or household anxieties, and to have their heart in heaven with the merciful God. Then you answer, "We lift them up to the Lord," assenting to it, by your avowal. But let no one come here, who could say with his mouth, "We lift up our hearts to the Lord," but in his thoughts his mind is concerned with the cares of this life. At

all times, rather, God should be in our memory; but if this is impossible by reason of human infirmity, in that hour above all this should be our earnest endeavor.

5 Then the Priest says, "Let us give thanks to the Lord." For verily we are bound to give thanks, that He called us, unworthy as we were, to so great grace; that He reconciled us when we were His foes; that He granted to us the Spirit of adoption. Then you say, "It is meet and right," for in giving thanks we do a meet thing and a right thing. But He did not just do right, but more than right, in doing us good and counting us for such great benefits.

THE ANAPHORA

Turning to the west, the priest signs the people once with the sign of the cross, saying:

PRIEST:
The Lord be with you all.

CONGREGATION:
And with your spirit.

The priest turns to the East and signs the deacons on his right once with the sign of the cross, saying:

PRIEST:
Lift up your hearts.

CONGREGATION:
We have them with the Lord.

The priest signs himself once with the sign of the cross, saying:

PRIEST:
Let us give thanks to the Lord.

CONGREGATION:
It is meet and right.

Editor's Commentary

In the Liturgy, the Church still retains this very ancient segment of the service, referred to as the "Anaphora," which is a Greek word (ἀναφορά) meaning "Lifting up," corresponding to the first declaration of the Priest to all present: "Lift up your hearts."

All the components of the Anaphora, and the responses back and forth, are present still in the Liturgy used in the church today, just as St. Cyril described it during his time.

6 After this, we make mention of heaven, and earth, and sea, of sun and moon, of stars and all the creation, rational and irrational, visible and invisible, of angels, archangels, virtues, dominions, principalities, powers, thrones,[1] of the Cherubim with many faces: in effect repeating that call of David's, "Magnify the Lord with me."[2] We make mention also of the Seraphim, whom Isaiah in the Holy Spirit saw standing around the throne of God, and with two of their wings covering their faces, and with two [wings covering] their feet, while with two they fly, crying "Holy, Holy, Holy, is the Lord of Sabaoth."[3] For the reason of our reciting this confession of God delivered down to us from the Seraphim, is this, that so we may be partakers with the hosts of the world above in their hymn of praise.

1 "For by Him all things were created that are in heaven and that are on earth, visible and invisible, whether thrones or dominions or principalities or powers. All things were created through Him and for Him" (Colossians 1:16).

2 Psalm 34:3

3 Isaiah 6:2–3. The term "Sabaoth" is derived originally from Aramaic, and refers to the angelic "hosts" (*saba* in Aramaic) of heaven.

ANAPHORA (CONTINUED)

PRIEST:
Meet and right, meet and right; truly, indeed, it is meet and right. O You, THE BEING, Master, Lord, God of Truth, being before the ages and reigning forever; who dwells in the highest and looks upon the lowly; who has created the heaven, the earth, the sea, and all that is therein; the Father of our Lord, God, and Savior Jesus Christ, by whom You have created all things, visible and invisible; who sits upon the throne of His glory; and who is worshiped by all the holy powers.

Editor's Commentary

In the Liturgy, just after the Anaphora as discussed above, the priest today does exactly as St. Cyril describes, mentioning how it is "meet and right" to lift up our hearts to God, the One who created all things: "the heaven, the earth, the sea, and all that is therein … the visible and invisible." The priest then reminds us of the throne of God and His glory, and how he is worshiped by "all the holy powers": angels, archangels, principalities, thrones, dominions, powers, the Cherubim,

Deacon:
You who are seated, stand.

Priest:
Before whom stand the angels, the archangels, the principalities, the authorities, the thrones, the dominions, and the powers.

Deacon:
Look towards the east.

Priest:
You are He around whom stand the cherubim full of eyes, and the seraphim with six wings, praising continuously, without ceasing, saying—

Deacon:
Let us attend.

Congregation:
The cherubim worship You, and the seraphim glorify You, proclaiming and saying, "Holy, holy, holy, Lord of hosts, heaven and earth are full of Your holy glory."

and the Seraphim.

Because, as St. Cyril states, we are being tasked with elevating our thoughts to consider ourselves "partakers with the [angelic] hosts of the world above in their hymn of praise," the deacon interposes an announcement to the congregation directing them to respond with the reverence due: (1) "You who are seated, stand." The priest replies by reminding everyone that before God "stand the angels," and so should we. (2) "Look towards the East." The priest responds mentioning the Cherubim who are "full of eyes" standing in reverence to God, and the Seraphim are "praising continuously, without ceasing." It is a call to all in attendance to be like the angels, looking attentively toward the altar and participating in the praise that is to come. And for this reason we have the third pronouncement from the deacon: (3) "Let us attend." In other words: be attentive as one should, if we were to imagine ourselves standing among the angels before the throne of God.

With such reverence, all in attendance are invited to chant the hymn of the Cherubim and the Seraphim, which St. Cyril makes mention of when he recalls Isaiah having seen them crying out "Holy Holy, Holy, Lord of Saboath [i.e., "hosts" of heaven]."

7 Then having sanctified ourselves by these spiritual hymns, we beseech the merciful God to send forth His Holy Spirit upon the gifts lying before Him; that He may make the bread the body of Christ, and the wine the blood of Christ; for

whatsoever the Holy Spirit has touched, is surely sanctified and changed.

HOLY, HOLY, HOLY

Priest:
Holy, holy, holy, indeed. O Lord our God, who formed us, created us, and placed us in the Paradise of joy, when we disobeyed Your commandment by the deceit of the serpent, we fell from eternal life and were exiled from the Paradise of joy. You have not abandoned us to the end, but have always visited us through Your holy prophets, and in the last days You manifested Yourself to us, who were sitting in darkness and the shadow of death, through Your only-begotten Son, our Lord, God, and Savior Jesus Christ, who, of the Holy Spirit and of the holy Virgin Mary—

Congregation:
Amen.

Priest:
was incarnate and became man, and taught us the ways of salvation. He granted us the birth from on high through water and Spirit. He made us unto Himself an assembled people, and sanctified us by Your Holy Spirit. He loved His own who are in the world, and gave Himself up as a ransom on our behalf, unto death, which reigned over us, whereby we were bound and sold on account of our sins. He descended into Hades through the cross.

Congregation:
Amen. I believe.

Priest:
He rose from the dead on the third day. He ascended into the heavens and sat at Your right hand, O Father.

Editor's Commentary

RECALLING THE STORY OF SALVATION

In the Liturgy, before approaching this segment which St. Cyril describes, the priest expounds on the holiness of God, and recalls the story of salvation: Humans were originally created and placed in the Paradise of Joy (also known as the Garden of Eden), disobeyed and were exiled from Paradise, then the Lord Christ manifested Himself to us through His incarnation of the Virgin St. Mary, and "loved His own who are in the world, and gave Himself up" for us "unto death," descending "into Hades, through the Cross" (Hades is where all individuals who died before Christ's salvation went; the righteous who believed in God awaited redemption from that dark abode, in order to be taken up to the heavenly Paradise to live with God); the priest then recalls the glorious resurrection and ascension, and the fact that we will all have to be subject to the judgment of God on judgment day, at which time God will "give each one according to His deeds." To wash away our sins and be prepared for the judgment, we must participate in the mystery of repentance and confess our sins and have them remitted, which is completed through the partaking of the true body and blood of the Lord.

He has appointed a Day for recompense, on which He will appear to judge the world in righteousness, and give each one according to his deeds.

Congregation:
According to Your mercy, O Lord, and not according to our sins.

THE INSTITUTION NARRATIVE

Priest:
He instituted for us this great Mystery of godliness. For being determined to give Himself up to death for the life of the world—

Congregation:
We believe.

Priest:
He took bread into His holy hands, which are without spot or blemish, blessed, and life-giving.

Congregation:
We believe that this is true. Amen.

Priest:
He looked up towards heaven to You, O God, who are His Father and Master of everyone.

Priest:
And when He had given thanks—

Congregation:
Amen.

Priest:
He blessed it—

Congregation:
Amen.

Priest:
He sanctified it.

Congregation:
We believe, we confess, and we glorify.

THE INSTITUTION NARRATIVE

Following this, we embark on a remembrance of how God "instituted for us this great Mystery of godliness"—that is, the mystery of His body and blood. This is, of course, in conformity with Christ's commandment: "Do this in remembrance of Me." (Luke 22:19. See also 1 Corinthians 11:17–34)

THE INVOCATION OF THE HOLY SPIRIT

In the Liturgy, after those two previous segments, we then come to what St. Cyril described: the invocation of the Holy Spirit to change the bread and wine into the body and blood of Christ. Because of this momentous mystery that we are about to experience, the deacon prefaces the prayers of the priest by announcing to all present: "Worship God in fear and trembling," followed thereafter with a call to attentiveness: "Let us attend."

The priest then prays inaudibly: "We ask You, O Lord our God … that Your Holy Spirit may descend upon us and upon these gifts set forth, and purify them, change them."

The priest follows this prayer by declaring aloud that this Mystery has been accomplished: "And this bread He makes into His holy body… And this cup also, [He makes into] the precious blood of His new covenant." The congregation replies by declaring their belief in the reality of this event, with each individually declaring while chanting altogether: "I believe. Amen."

Priest:
He broke it, and gave it to His own holy disciples and saintly apostles, saying, "Take, eat of it, all of you. For this is My body, which is broken for you and for many, to be given for the remission of sins. This do in remembrance of Me."

Congregation:
This is true. Amen.

Priest:
Likewise also, the cup, after supper, He mixed it of wine and water. And when He had given thanks—

Congregation:
Amen.

Priest:
He blessed it—

Congregation:
Amen.

Priest:
He sanctified it.

Congregation:
Again, we believe, we confess, and we glorify.

Priest:
He tasted, and gave it also to His own holy disciples and saintly apostles, saying, "Take, drink of it, all of you. For this is My blood of the New Covenant, which is shed for you and for many, to be given for the remission of sins. This do in remembrance of Me."

Congregation:
This is also true. Amen.

Priest:
"For every time you eat of this bread and drink of this cup, you proclaim My Death, confess My Resurrection, and remember Me till I come."

Congregation:
Amen. Amen. Amen. Your Death, O Lord, we proclaim; Your holy Resurrection and Ascension [into the heavens,] we confess. We praise You, we bless You, we thank You, O Lord, and we entreat You, O our God.

Priest:
Therefore, as we also commemorate His holy Passion, His Resurrection from the dead, His Ascension into the heavens, His Sitting at Your right hand, O Father, and His Second Coming from the heavens, awesome and full of glory, we offer unto You Your gifts from what is Yours, for everything, concerning everything, and in everything.

Deacon:
Worship God in fear and trembling.

While all the people bow their heads, they say:

Congregation:
We praise You, we bless You, we serve You, we worship You.

While kneeling with outstretched hands, the priest says the Prayer of the Descent of the Holy Spirit (the Epiclesis) inaudibly:

Priest:
And we ask You, O Lord our God—we Your sinful and unworthy servants, we worship You by the pleasure of Your goodness—that Your Holy Spirit may descend,

He points to himself with his hands and then to the oblations present before him and says:

upon us and upon these gifts set forth, and purify them, change them, and manifest them as a sanctification of Your saints.

Deacon:
Let us attend. Amen.

Three times the priest quickly signs with the sign of the cross the oblation which is upon the paten, and says aloud:

Priest:
And this bread He makes into His holy body.

Congregation:
I believe. Amen.

The priest stretches out his hands and bows his head to the Lord, saying:

Priest:
Our Lord, God, and Savior Jesus Christ, given for the remission of sins and eternal life to those who partake of Him.

Three times, the priest quickly signs the chalice with the sign of the cross.

Priest:
And this cup also, the precious blood of His new covenant.

Congregation:
Again, I believe.

The priest stretches out his hands and bows his head to the Lord, saying:

Priest:
Our Lord, God, and Savior Jesus Christ, given for the remission of sins and eternal life to those who partake of Him.

Now indeed the bread has become the body of Christ and the wine the blood of Christ. After this, the signings of both of them shall be through them and by them:

Congregation:
Amen. Lord have mercy. Lord have mercy. Lord have mercy.

8 Then, after the spiritual sacrifice, the bloodless service, is completed, over that sacrifice of propitiation we entreat God for the common peace of the churches, for the welfare of the world, for kings, for soldiers and allies, for the sick, for the afflicted, and, in a word, for all who stand in need of support we all pray and offer this sacrifice.

Editor's Commentary

We do exactly this in the Liturgy. The Holy Spirit having descended on the bread and wine, and they having been changed into the body and blood of our Lord, it is as if the "king" just entered, and we are now petitioning the king for support for various aspects of our lives.

We pray seven litanies:

1) The peace of the church

2) The archbishop and bishops

3) The hegumens, priests, deacons, subdeacons
4) The servants and all the faithful generally
5) Safety (salvation) and welfare of the world
6) The nourishment and fruitfulness of the land
7) The precious gifts, sacrifices, and those who brought them.

In other liturgies used by the Coptic Church, we pray also regarding a number of matters, including for our Christ-loving leaders, soldiers and those in the government, those in captivity, the sick, widows, and orphans.

9 Then we commemorate also those who have fallen asleep before us, first Patriarchs, Prophets, Apostles, Martyrs, that at their prayers and intercessions God would receive our petition. Then on behalf also of the Holy Fathers and Bishops who have fallen asleep before us, and in a word of all who in past years have fallen asleep among us, believing that it will be a very great benefit to the souls, for whom the supplication is put up, while that holy and most awesome sacrifice is set forth.

10 And I wish to persuade you by an illustration, for I know that many say, "What is a soul profited, which departs from this world either with sins, or without sins, if it be commemorated in the prayer?" If a king were to banish certain people who had given him offense, and then those who belong to them should weave a crown and offer it to him on behalf of those under punishment, would he not grant a remission of their penalties? In the same way we, when we offer to Him our supplications for those who have fallen asleep, though they be sinners, we weave no crown, but offer up Christ sacrificed for our sins, propitiating our merciful God for them as well as for ourselves.

THE COMMEMORATION OF THE SAINTS

Priest:

As this, O Lord, is the command of Your only-begotten Son, that we share in the commemoration of Your saints, graciously accord, O Lord, to remember all the saints who have pleased You since the beginning: our holy fathers the patriarchs, the prophets, the apostles, the preachers, the evangelists, the martyrs, the confessors, and all the spirits of the righteous perfected in the faith. Most of all, the pure, full-of-glory, ever-virgin, holy Theotokos, Saint Mary, who truly gave birth to God the Logos. And Saint John the forerunner, baptist, and martyr; Saint Stephen the archdeacon and protomartyr; the beholder-of-God, Saint Mark the Evangelist, the apostle and martyr; the patriarch Saint Severus; our teacher Dioscorus; Saint Athanasius the Apostolic; Saint Peter, the holy martyr and high priest; Saint John Chrysostom; Saint Theodosius; Saint Theophilus; Saint Demetrius; Saint Cyril; Saint Basil; Saint Gregory the Theologian; Saint Gregory the Wonderworker; Saint Gregory the Armenian; the three hundred and eighteen assembled at Nicea; the one hundred and fifty at Constantinople; and the two hundred at Ephesus; our righteous father, the great Abba Anthony; the righteous Abba Paul; the three saints Abba Macarii and all their children, the cross-bearers; our father Abba John the hegumen; our righteous father Abba Pishoy, the perfect man, the beloved of our good Savior.... and all the choir of Your saints, through whose prayers and supplications have mercy on us all and save us, for the sake of Your holy name, which is called upon us.

Editor's Commentary

Here too we find the striking similarity to what is in the Liturgy today. After the litanies are prayed, the priest commemorates the departed, in the same order. We recite the bishops who have fallen asleep, and many other saints. Interestingly you will find St. Cyril mention two reasons for this commemoration of the departed: for our benefit ("that at their prayers and intercessions God would receive our petition), and for their benefit ("believe it will be a very great benefit to the souls.").

In the Liturgy we see the same: *For our benefit*: The priest prays to God regarding the "choir of all Your saints, through whose prayers and supplications [we hope for God to] have mercy on us all and save us." In the liturgy of St. Cyril (of Alexandria), also often referred to as the liturgy of St. Mark, the priest prays the following, after commemorating the departed: "Not that we are worthy, O Master, to intercede for the blessedness of those who are there, but rather they are standing before the tribunal of Your only-begotten Son, that they may be instead interceding for our poverty and our frailty. May You be a forgiver of our iniquities, for the sake of their holy supplications and for the sake of Your blessed name which is called upon us." *For their benefit*: We find the deacon, and the priest, pray for the "repose" of their souls in the Paradise of Joy. **St. John Chrysostom** says something similarly: "For not unmeaningly have these things been devised, nor do we in vain make mention of the

* * *

Graciously, O Lord, repose all their souls in the bosom of our holy fathers Abraham, Isaac, and Jacob, sustain them in green pastures, beside still waters in the Paradise of joy, the place out of which grief, sorrow, and groaning have fled away in the light of Your saints.

* * *

Those, O Lord, whose souls You have taken, repose them in the Paradise of joy, in the region of the living forever, in the heavenly Jerusalem—in that place. And we too, who are sojourners in this place, keep us in Your faith, and grant us Your peace unto the end.

departed in the course of the divine mysteries, and approach God on their behalf, beseeching the Lamb who is before us, who takes away the sin of the world. Not in vain, but that some refreshment may thereby ensue to them. Not in vain does he that stand by the altar cry out when the tremendous mysteries are celebrated, for all that have fallen asleep in Christ, and for those who perform commemorations on their behalf. For if there were no commemorations for them, these things would not have been spoken, since our service is not a mere stage show, God forbid! Yes, it is by the ordinance of the Spirit that these things are said. Let us then give them aid and perform commemoration for them."[1] **St. Epiphanius of Salamis** states: "Useful ... is the prayer fashioned on their behalf, even if it does not force back the whole of guilty charges laid to them. And it is useful also, because in this world we often stumble either voluntarily or involuntarily, and thus it is a reminder to do better."[2] **His Holiness Pope Shenouda III** echoed similar sentiments: "[We pray for the departed] so that he could at least depart from the world having been absolved by the Church, so that he is no longer bound in any way. That person is then left to the mercy of the One who searches men's hearts and the One who knows all secrets. It is as if the Church is saying to God, 'This person has been released from our side by the authority to loose and bind which You gave us [cf. Mt 18:18; Jn 20:23], and so we leave him now to Your mercy and to Your knowledge which is beyond ours.' The Church also prays on behalf of the one who is passing on, for him to be forgiven any sins which he may have committed which were not of the degree that leads to death [cf. 1 Jn 5:16–17]. So what are these sins that do not lead to death? They are uncompleted sins, sins that have not been fully carried out. They [also] may be sins of ignorance, sins committed unintentionally, or sins that are latent, or sins of negligence, for example.... Let us suppose that a person has died suddenly without having had a chance to confess, or that he has forgotten to confess some sins, and therefore has not received an absolution for them. The Church can give him absolution and asks forgiveness for him, in the Prayer for the Departed."[3]

1 Homily 41 on 1 Corinthians (NPNF[1] 12).

2 Epiphanius Salamis *Against All Heresies* 75.8. In William A. Jurgens, *The Faith of the Early Fathers* 2 (Collegeville, MN: The Liturgical Press, 1979), 76.

3 H.H. Pope Shenouda III, *Many Years with the People's Questions, Part IV* (El Kawmia, Cairo, Egypt: Dar El Tebaa, 1993), 32–35

11 Then, after these things, we say that Prayer which the Savior delivered to His own disciples, with a pure conscience giving God the title "our Father," and saying: **"Our Father, who art in heaven."** O most surpassing loving-kindness of God! On them who revolved from Him and were in the very extreme of misery has He bestowed such a complete forgiveness of evil deeds, and so great a participation of grace, so that they should even call Him "Father." "Our Father, who art in heaven"—and they also are a "heaven," those who bear the image of the heavenly,[1] in whom is God, dwelling and walking in them.[2]

12 **"Hallowed be Thy name."** The name of God is in its nature holy, whether we say it or not; but since it is sometimes profaned among sinners—according to the words, "Through you My name is continually blasphemed among the Gentiles"[3]—we pray that in us God's name may be hallowed, not that it becomes holy from not being holy, but because it becomes holy in us, when we are made holy, and do things worthy of holiness.

13 **"Thy kingdom come."** A pure soul can say with boldness, "Thy kingdom come," for he who has heard Paul saying, "Therefore do not let sin reign in your mortal body,"[4] and

1 "And as we have borne the image of the *man* of dust, we shall also bear the image of the heavenly Man" (1 Corinthians 15:49).

2 "And what agreement has the temple of God with idols? For you are the temple of the living God. As God has said: 'I will dwell in them, and walk among them. I will be their God, and they shall be My people'" (2 Corinthians 6:16).

3 "For 'the name of God is blasphemed among the Gentiles because of you,' as it is written" (Romans 2:24). "... My name is blasphemed continually every day" (Isaiah 52:5).

4 Romans 6:12

has cleansed himself in deed, and thought, and word, will say to God, "Thy kingdom come."

14 **"Thy will be done, on earth as it is in heaven."** God's divine and blessed angels do the will of God, as David said in the Psalm, "Bless the Lord, all you His angels, mighty in strength, who do His word."[1] So then in effect you mean this by your prayer: "As it is for the Angels that Your will is done, so likewise may it be done on earth in me, O Lord."

15 **"Give us this day our substantial bread."** Common bread is not substantial[2] bread, but this holy bread is substantial—

1 Psalm 103:20

2 Instead of the commonly translated word "daily," the word "substance" is one that is frequently used by discerning translators of the Lord's Prayer. The specific word in Greek, ἐπιούσιον (*epiousion*), is a form of Greek that is written in a "common dialect" (Koine Greek). The word occurs only in two places in the Septuagint, with both passages being the Lord's Prayer (in Matthew 6:11 and Luke 11:3). Given this, its interpretation often relies upon studying the word itself, and analyzing its parts and associated context. The term "epi" means "on top of," and "ousion" means "substance: or "being." So the phrase is then often translated as "substantial" or "super-substantial" bread: more-than-necessary bread. In the first Latin translation of the Lord's Prayer, by St. Jerome, it was translated *panem supersubstantionem,* and then at some point it was later translated to *cotidianum* (which in Latin means "daily"). "Super-substantial" or "substantial" bread is often interpreted by as being the bread for the coming age, "Give us today the bread of tomorrow." Thus, generally speaking, Church Fathers often interpret this petition as not being for common bread of every day life, but for spiritual food, and often a reference to the Holy Eucharist. Even if one were to include in their interpretation of this term the notion of this being common bread for physical nourishment, the Fathers warn we should acknowledge this petition as also referring to the heavenly bread, who is Christ our Savior. Let us remember that the Lord taught us not to seek the bread that perishes, but the bread that when you eat it you will not die ("Do not labor for the food which perishes, but for the food which endures to everlasting life, which the Son of Man will give you, because God the Father has set His seal on Him" [John 6:27]), and so it makes sense that this Lord's Prayer is one that points to the heavenly bread (see John 6).

that is, appointed for the substance of the soul; for this bread goes into the belly and is cast out into the draught.

16 **"And forgive us our debts as we also forgive our debtors."** For we have many sins; for we offend both in word and in thought, and very many things we do that is worthy of condemnation; and "if we say that we have no sin," we lie, as John says.[1] And we make a covenant with God, entreating Him to forgive us our sins, as we also forgive our neighbors their debts. Considering then what we receive, and in return for what, let us not put off nor delay to forgive one another. The offenses committed against us are slight and trivial, and easily settled; but those which we have committed against God are great, and need such mercy as is only [found in] Him. Take heed therefore, lest for the slight and trivial sins against you, that you shut out for yourself forgiveness from God for your very grievous sins.[2]

17 **"And lead us not into temptation, O Lord."** Is this then what the Lord teaches us to pray, that we may not be tempted at all? How then is it said elsewhere, "a man who is not tempted, is a man unproven";[3] and again, "My brethren, count it all

---

1 "If we say that we have no sin, we deceive ourselves, and the truth is not in us" (1 John 1:8).

2 See the Parable of the Unforgiving Servant in Matthew 18:21–35, which illustrates this warning

3 While there is not a specific verse that states this exactly, we can read a similar message in James 1:12–13, 2 Corinthians 13:5–7. Tertullian expresses something akin to this: "For the word had gone before, "that no one not tempted should attain to the celestial kingdoms" (On Baptism, Chapter 20). Likewise, we read in the Apostolic Constitutions: "The Scripture says, 'A man that is a reprobate [unprincipled] is not tried by God'" (2.8).

joy when you fall into various trials."[1] But, perhaps, does the entering into temptation mean the being overwhelmed by the temptation? For temptation is, as it were, like a winter torrent difficult to cross. Those therefore who are not overwhelmed in temptations pass through, showing themselves as being excellent swimmers, and not being swept away by them at all, while those who are not such, enter into them and are overwhelmed. As for example Judas, having entered into the temptation of the love of money, did not swim through it, but was overwhelmed and was strangled both in body and spirit. Peter entered into the temptation of the denial, but having entered, he was not overwhelmed by it, but courageously swam through it and was delivered from the temptation. Listen again, in another place, to a company of unscathed saints, giving thanks for deliverance from temptation:

You, O God, have tested us; You have refined us as silver is refined. You brought us into the net; You laid affliction on our loins. You have caused men to ride over our heads; we went through fire and water; but You brought us out into a place of rest.[2] You see them speaking boldly in regard to their having passed through and not been pierced. "But you brought us out into a place of rest"; now their coming into a place of rest is their being delivered from temptation.

18 **"But deliver us from evil."** If "Lead us not into temptation" implied not being tempted at all, He would not have said, "But deliver us from evil." Now, evil is our adversary the devil, from whom we pray to be delivered. Then, after completing

1 James 1:2

2 Psalm 66:10–12

the prayer you say, "Amen." By this "Amen," which means "so be it," you set your seal to the petitions of the divinely-taught prayer."

THE FRACTION PRAYERS

While breaking the holy body, the priest says the following Prayer of the Fraction (or one of the other appointed fraction prayers).

Priest:
O Master, Lord our God, the Great, the Eternal, who are wondrous in glory; Who keeps His covenant and His mercy to those who love Him with all their heart; who has given to us redemption of sins through His only-begotten Son, Jesus Christ our Lord, the life of everyone, the help of those who flee to Him, the hope of those who cry out to Him; before whom stand thousands of thousands and ten thousand times ten thousands holy angels and archangels, the cherubim and the seraphim, and all the innumerable host of the heavenly powers. O God, You have sanctified these gifts which are set forth through the coming down upon them of Your Holy Spirit; You have purified them. Purify us also, our Master, from our sins, the hidden and manifest; and every thought which is not pleasing to Your goodness, O God, the Lover of Mankind, may it be far from us. Purify our souls, our bodies, our spirits, our hearts, our eyes, our understanding, our thoughts, and our consciences, so that, with a pure heart, an enlightened soul, an unashamed countenance, a faith unfeigned, a perfect love, and a firm hope, we may dare with boldness, without fear, to pray to You, O God, the holy Father who are in the heavens, and say:
"Our Father ..."

Editor's Commentary

According to St. Cyril, immediatly after the "supplications for those who have fallen asleep," the congregation would then pray the Lord's prayer. In modern times, the Coptic rite includes a prayer inserted between them known as "The Prayer of the Fraction," during which the priest fractions the holy body. The actual text of the Fraction Prayers are variable, determined based on what is being commemorated on that day of the Liturgy. For example, there are prayers for different feasts (Nativity, Theophany, Hosanna Sunday, Resurrection), prayers during certain fasts (the Great Fast before Resurrection, the Apostle's Fast which culminates with commemorating the martyrdom of St. Peter and St. Paul).

At the conclusion of every Fraction Prayer, just before the priest directs the congregation to pray the Lord's prayer, the priest expresses the same sentiment each time, conveying, as St. Cyril described it, "so great a participation of grace, so that [we] should even call Him "Father." Compare that to the priest's prayers: "with ... a firm hope, we may dare with boldness, without fear, to pray to You, ... and say: 'Our Father ...'"

19 After this the Priest says, "Holy things to holy men." Holy are the gifts presented, having received the visitation of the Holy Spirit. Holy are you also, having been deemed worthy of the Holy Spirit; the holy things therefore correspond to holy persons. Then you say, "One is Holy, one is the Lord Jesus Christ." For one is truly, by nature holy; we too are holy, but not by nature, only by participation, and discipline, and prayer.

PRIEST:

O Master, Lord God the Pantocrator, the healer of our souls, bodies, and spirits ... let Your servants, my fathers and my brethren and my own weakness, be absolved by my mouth, through Your Holy Spirit, O Good One and Lover of Mankind. O God, who takes away the sin of the world, hasten to accept the repentance of Your servants, for a light of knowledge and forgiveness of sins. For You are a compassionate and merciful God; You are patient; Your mercy is great and true. If we have sinned against You, either by word or by deeds, pardon and forgive us, as a Good One and Lover of Mankind. O God, absolve us, and absolve all Your people....

Remember, O Lord, our assemblies; bless them.

The deacon raises the cross, and says:

DEACON:

Saved. Amen. And with your spirit. In the fear of God, let us attend.

CONGREGATION:

Amen. Lord have mercy. Lord have mercy. Lord have mercy.

The priest takes in his hands the Despotikon and raises it up to arm's length, and with bowed head he exclaims aloud:

Editor's Commentary

In the Liturgy, the priest says "The Holies are for the holy." To approach the Eucharist, one must have received the Holy Spirit, which is granted to those who are baptized. Thus, it makes sense what St. Cyril says, that they are holy who have been "deemed worthy of the Holy Spirit." But even more than that, one must approach the Eucharist worthily, which St. Cyril further elaborates on: "We too are holy, but not by nature, only by participation, and discipline, and prayer." We begin our life with God and are given a new spiritual birth to live a spiritual life through the Holy Spirit. The Holy Spirit continues to participate with us during our lives, aiding us in our prayers, as well as our efforts to discipline ourselves (striving in life to be godly). The Holy Spirit thus leads us to live a life of holiness that allows us to approach the Eucharist.

Having declared then that "The Holies are for the holy," just before the people respond to this proclamation indicating that only one is truly Holy by nature (as St.

PRIEST:
The Holies for the holy.

The people worship before the Lord with fear and trembling, praying for the forgiveness of their sins with tears and supplication. Then the priest takes the Despotikon, signs (in the form of a cross) the blood inside, soaks its extremity and signs the body, then blood in the chalice again, then carefully places the Despotikon upside down in the blood inside the chalice, all the while with his left hand cupped under the Despotikon lest any of the pearls should fall or drip, while saying:

Blessed be the Lord Jesus Christ, the Son of God; the sanctification is by the Holy Spirit. Amen.

CONGREGATION:
One is the holy Father, one is the holy Son, one is the Holy Spirit. Amen.

PRIEST:
Peace be with all.

CONGREGATION:
And with your spirit.

Cyril mentions is the rite), the priest takes the central portion[*] of the holy body, signs with it the precious blood inside the chalice in the form of a cross, and eventually places it upside down into the chalice, while declaring: "Blessed be the Lord Jesus Christ, the Son of God, the sanctification is by the Holy Spirit. Amen." Here we see an echo of what St. Cyril indicates, that "the gifts presented" are "holy" for "having receiving the visitation of the Holy Spirit"; likewise, the priest in the Liturgy says "sanctification is by the Holy Spirit."

It is after this that the congregation respond, but instead of simply saying "the Lord Jesus Christ" is holy, the response is broadened to encompass the triune God: "One is the holy Father, one is the holy Son, one is the Holy Spirit. Amen." This aligns more closely with the Apostolic Constitutions (8.13) which states: "Let the Bishop speak thus to the people: 'Holy things for holy persons.' And let the people answer, 'There is one that is holy, there is one Lord, one Jesus Christ, blessed forever, to the glory of God the Father.'" Ancient manuscripts of the Liturgy attributed to St. Mark the Evangelist shows even more similarity: "One Father holy, one Son holy, one Spirit holy, in the unity of the Holy Spirit."

[*] This is referred to in the Coptic Church by the term "Despoticon" (also often spelled "Despotikon"), which is a derivative from the Greek word for "Lord" or "Master."

20 After this you hear the chanter inviting you with a sacred melody to the communion of the Holy Mysteries, and saying,

"O taste and see that the Lord is good."[1] Do not trust your bodily palate's judgment; no, rather your unfaltering faith, for they who taste are asked to taste, not bread and wine, but the antitypical[2] body and blood of Christ.

---

1 Psalm 34:8

2 An "antitype" refers to something foreshadowed beforehand. In this instance, St. Cyril is referring to the body and blood of Christ as having been prefigured in the Old Testament (i.e., there were symbols or types in the Old Testament that were foreshadowing the body and blood of Christ that we now have in the Eucharist).

THE CONFESSION

Priest:
The holy body and the precious, true blood of Jesus Christ, the Son of our God. Amen.

Congregation:
Amen.

Priest:
The holy, precious body and the true blood of Jesus Christ, the Son of our God. Amen.

Congregation:
Amen.

Priest:
The body and the blood of Immanuel our God; this is true. Amen.

Congregation:
Amen. I believe.

Priest:
Amen. Amen. Amen. I believe, I believe, I believe and confess to the last breath that this is the life-giving Flesh that Your only-begotten Son, our Lord, God, and Savior Jesus Christ, took from our Lady, the Lady of us all, the holy Theotokos, Saint Mary. He made It one with His divinity without mingling, without confusion, and without alteration.

Editor's Commentary

In the Liturgy, before the distribution of the Mysteries, the priest, deacon, and congregation, all confess "unfaltering faith," as St. Cyril says, that this is not just bread and wine, but truly the "body and blood of Christ." Three times the priest declares this, and the people each time respond "Amen" and in the final response they add an individual confession: "I believe." The priest then confesses, "to the last breath that this is the life-giving flesh"[1] of Christ, that was taken from St. Mary in His incarnation and "made it one with His divinity without mingling, without confusion, and without alteration."[2] He goes on to declare, "Truly I believe that His divinity parted not from His humanity for a single moment, nor a twinkling of an eye."[3] The priest concludes by emphatically confessing: "I believe, I believe, I believe that this is true Amen." The deacon then echoes the confession of the priest and declares aloud from the altar table, "Amen.

He confessed the good confession before Pontius Pilate. He gave It up for us upon the holy wood of the Cross, of His own will, for us all. Truly I believe that His divinity parted not from His humanity for a single moment, nor a twinkling of an eye; given for us for salvation, remission of sins, and eternal life to those who partake of Him. I believe, I believe, I believe that this is true. Amen.

Deacon:

Amen. Amen. Amen. I believe, I believe, I believe that this is true. Amen. Pray for us and for all Christians who said to us concerning them, "Remember us [in the house of the Lord]." The peace and love of Jesus Christ be with you. Let us sing, "Alleluia." Pray for the worthy partaking of the immaculate and heavenly Holy Mysteries. Lord have mercy.

While bearing the paten with the body of Christ, the priest begins distributing the Holy Mysteries to the people by turning to the west and, with the paten, blessing the people with the sign of the cross, saying:

Priest:

The Holies for the holy. Blessed be the Lord Jesus Christ the Son of God; the sanctification is by the Holy Spirit. Amen.

All the people, along with the deacons, bow, saying:

Congregation:

Blessed is He who comes in the name of the Lord.

THE DISTRIBUTION OF THE HOLY MYSTERIES

During the distribution of the Holy Mysteries, the people chant Psalm 150. Then the congregation chants what is appropriate for the day.

Amen. Amen. I believe, I believe, I believe that this is true. Amen." He concludes his confession directing the congregation to "pray for the worthy partaking of the immaculate and heavenly, holy Mysteries."

It is only after these confessions that a "melody to the communion" (as St. Cyril says) is chanted during the distribution of the Eucharist. While St. Cyril refers to Psalm 34:8 as the content of that melody,[4] in the Coptic Rite the Liturgical melody chanted is from another psalm: Psalm 150.

In the Apostolic Constitutions we read of the rite as follows: before distribution of the Mysteries, the people declare "Glory to God in the highest, and on earth peace, good-will among men. Hosanna to the son of David! Blessed be He that comes in the name of the Lord, being the Lord God who appeared to us, Hosanna in the highest."[5] In the Coptic rite, when the priest finishes the initial distribution of the body to those serving the altar, and he is about to distribute to the people, he lifts the body while covered in the paten, declaring as he did earlier before the Confession: "The Holies for the holy. Blessed be the Lord Jesus Christ the Son of God; the sanctification is by the Holy Spirit. Amen." And the people respond similarly as noted in the Apostolic Constitutions, "Blessed is He who comes in the name of the Lord."

1 The word "life-giving" was added to the Confession prayer by the 72nd Pope of the Coptic Church, Pope Youannis V, in the 12th

Century (see Synaxarion entry for the 4th of Bashans).

2 The 70th Pope of the Coptic Church, Pope Gabriel, added "He made it one with His divinity" to the Confession Prayer. Then, in order not to confuse people into thinking this means the divinity of the Lord Christ intermingled with or altered His humanity, the bishops of the Coptic Church further added this second portion of this prayer "without mingling, without confusion, and without alteration," to avoid any semblance to the heresy of Eutyches (a priest who first came to notice in the third ecumenical council at Ephesus in AD 431, whose teachings [Christ was a "fusion of human and divine elements"] were condemned in the Council of Chalcedon in AD 451).

3 Many declarations and statements have been made in recent years among different ancient denominations of Christianity, specifically referring to this confession as "a common formula expressing our official agreement on Christology" (as declared by the Dialogue between the Catholic and the Coptic Church in 1988, following the joint declaration of Pope of Rome Paul VI, and the Coptic Pope of Alexandria Shenouda III in 1973); later joint statements among the Eastern and Oriental Orthodox (1989, and later in 1990) have echoed these sentiments as indicative of a "common faith and continuous loyalty to the Apostolic Tradition that should be the basis for our unity and communion" (1990 Joint Commission of The Theological Dialogue Between The Orthodox Church And The Oriental Orthodox Churches, Second Agreed Statement).

4 The *Apostolic Constitutions* (8.14) indicates all of Psalm 34 is chanted while people are partaking of communion.

5 *Apostolic Constitutions* 8.13

21 In approaching therefore, come not with your wrists extended, or your fingers spread; but make your left hand a throne for the right, as for that which is to receive a king. And having hollowed your palm, receive the body of Christ, saying over it, "Amen." So then after having carefully made holy your eyes by the touch of the holy body, partake of it, paying attention for fear that you lose any portion of it, because whatever you lose is evidently a loss to you as it were from one of your own members [of your own body]. For tell me, if anyone gave you grains of gold, would you not hold them with all carefulness, being on guard against losing any of them and suffering loss? Will you then much more carefully keep watch that not a crumb fall from you from what is more precious than gold and precious stones?

22 Then after you have partaken of the body of Christ, draw near, draw near also to the cup of Christ, not stretching forth your hands, but bending; and saying with an air of worship and reverence, "Amen," make yourself holy by partaking also of the blood of Christ. And while the moisture is still upon your lips, touch it with your hands, and make holy your eyes and brow and the other organs of sense. Then wait for the prayer and giving thanks unto God, who has accounted you worthy of such great mysteries.

Editor's Commentary

Today, during the distribution of the Holy Mysteries, the remarkable reverence due while partaking of the body and blood of Christ is still evident.

Whereas in St. Cyril's time the communicant appears to have been customarily permitted, with reverence, to touch the body, holding it in their hand, and even being encouraged by St. Cyril to touch the blood that is on one's lips, in the Coptic tradition today we find reverence to the extent that the communicant (other than a member of clergy) is not permitted to touch the Eucharist by hand. Instead, a person is typically asked to take a square linen and drape it over their right hand, and have the priest place the body directly in the person's mouth, with the covered hand serving as simply a safeguard in case any of the precious jewels were to fall (and if they did, they would not be caught in the bare hand; even if a piece of the body were to fall on the ground, typically those around the priest would simply point it out and have the priest himself be the one to pick it up by his bare hands). The traditional practice in the Coptic Church while partaking of the blood also dictates not touching the blood, the chalice, or the spoon even, with one's hand, but instead to have the priest place the spoon, with the blood in it, directly into the mouth of the communicant; if anything were to drip on some cloth, for example, the typical direction given would be for the priest to wash it with water over the paten, followed by drinking the water that falls into the paten.[1]

Today, as each communicant approaches to partake of the body and the blood, they will typically hear the priest saying, "This is truly the body/blood of Immanuel our God. Amen,"[2] and as St. Cyril attests to the practice at his time, each communicant is expected to say "Amen," to confirm their personal belief with "unfaltering faith."[3]

After one has partaken of communion, there are a set of personal prayers commonly made available to thank God for being granted the grace of partaking of the Holy Mysteries, aligned with what St. Cyril mentions happens: "giving thanks unto God who has accounted you worthy of such great mysteries." Those personal prayers of thanks after communion are similar to what we find in the Apostolic Constitutions, which elaborates on the gratitude communicants should feel, as follows: "Now we have received the precious body and the precious blood of Christ, let us give thanks to Him who has thought us worthy to partake of these His holy mysteries; and let us beseech Him that it may not be to us for condemnation, but for salvation, to the advantage of soul and body, to the preservation of piety, to the remission of sins, and to the life of the world to come. Let us arise, and by the grace of Christ let us dedicate ourselves to God, to the only unbegotten God, and to His Christ."[4]

The priest then proceeds to ensure all of the body and blood have been consumed before concluding the service.[5]

---

1 Origen remarks on the care and reverence shown: "I wish to admonish you by examples from your own religion. You who have been accustomed to attend the Sacred Mysteries, know how, when you receive the body of the Lord, you guard it with all care and reverence, that no little part of it fall down, no portion of the consecrated gift slip away. For you believe yourselves guilty, and rightly so believe, if any part of it falls through carelessness." (Homily 133 on Exodus, part 3)

2 In the *Apostolic Constitutions* (8.23), we read: "And let the bishop give the oblation, saying, "The body of Christ"; and let him that receives say, "Amen." And let the deacon [of the rank of the clergy] take the cup; and when he gives it, say, "The blood of Christ, the cup of life"; and let him that drinks say, "Amen."

3 Lecture 23.20

4 *Apostolic Constitutions* 8.24

5 In the fourteenth century commentary of Abu'l Bircat on the Coptic Liturgy, we read with reference to the consumption of the remains: "And when he has completed these things with regard to the distribution of the communion, the priest will take care that if by chance any small particle however small of the body be left over he gather it up and give it to those ministering at the altar. Let the deacon also bear away the chalice in which the priest has communicated with the Despoticon [the central portion of the body], and likewise the blood if any of it be left over." *The Treatment of the Remains of the Eucharist After Holy Communion and the Time of the Ablutions*, W. Lockton, London, Cambridge University Press, 1920), 23.

23 Hold fast these traditions unaltered, and keep yourselves free from offense. Do not sever yourselves from the Communion. Do not deprive yourselves through the pollution of sins, of these Holy and Spiritual Mysteries. "And may the God of peace sanctify you completely, and may your spirit, soul, and body be entirely preserved blameless at the coming of our Lord Jesus Christ"[1]—to whom be glory and honor and might, with the Father and the Holy Spirit, now and forever, and unto the ages of ages. Amen.

1 1 Thessalonians 5:23

Editor's Commentary

Here we see a reminder of this notion of partaking of Communion worthily. As is followed in modern times, so we see St. Cyril making it clear that "through the pollution of sins" one may be deprived of being allowed to partake of the Holy Mysteries. As St. Cyril states, the Eucharist is sought for the forgiveness of sins, and we ask also for sanctification of our spirit, soul, and body, as a defense to aid us at the Judgment Day when the Lord Christ comes again. We can hear a similar prayer in the Liturgy in the Fraction Prayer, to the Father: "Make us worthy to partake of Your ineffable good things, for the salvation of our souls, bodies, and spirits, and for a defense before Your fearful tribunal."

www.ingramcontent.com/pod-product-compliance
Lightning Source LLC
Chambersburg PA
CBHW020952030426
42339CB00004B/62